Helen Wilhelmina Ludlow, R. H Hamilton

Tuskegee Normal and Industrial School

Helen Wilhelmina Ludlow, R. H Hamilton

Tuskegee Normal and Industrial School

ISBN/EAN: 9783337005689

Printed in Europe, USA, Canada, Australia, Japan

Cover: Foto ©Andreas Hilbeck / pixelio.de

More available books at **www.hansebooks.com**

TUSKEGEE, ALABAMA.

BOOKER T. WASHINGTON, Principal.

OLIVIA A. DAVIDSON, Ass't. Principal.

ITS STORY AND ITS SONGS.

.

EDITED BY HELEN W. LUDLOW,

OF HAMPTON INSTITUTE.

NORMAL SCHOOL STEAM PRESS,

Hampton, Va.

1884.

.

Printed by Colored and Indian
Students at Hampton Institute, Va.

THE STORY OF TUSKEGEE.

A STORY OF PROGRESS, PLUCK AND PROVIDENCE.

Fourteen years ago, in 1870, it is said, Northern teachers in the
South for the purpose of teaching colored schools, were frightened
away by the whites from the town of Tuskegee, Alabama. Four
years ago, the member of the Alabama Legislature from Tuskegee,
a prominent democrat and present Speaker of the House, offered a
bill which was passed by the General Assembly, appropriating $2000
annually to pay the salaries of teachers in a Normal School to be located at Tuskegee for the training of colored teachers.

The Act of Assembly being approved in February, 1881, the State
Superintendent of Educ tion in Alabama wrote to Gen. S. C. Armstrong, Principal of the Hampton Normal and Agricultural Institute,
Virginia, requesting him to nominate a fit person for Principal of the
new school. He recommended Mr. Booker T. Washington of West
Virginia, a graduate of Hampton Institute, class of '75, who, after two
years' teaching of his people in his own state, had been put in charge
of its Indian boys and had shown abilities of a very high order for
such a position. Mr. Washington was appointed and at once entered
upon his work. Arriving on the ground, he found no well appointed
school-house ready for him or any prospect of one. The State appro-
priated money only to pay the salaries of the principal and teachers,
nothing for school-building, or outfit of furniture, books and appara-
tus, or current expenses. For all these the colored people themselves were to provide, if they would take advantage of the State's as-
sistance. One week remained to prepare for the opening of the Normal School. The new Principal utilized it in surveying the field to
see what need and encouragement for one existed.

Tuskegee is a beautiful little town, with a high and healthy situation and such as is rarely seen in the South, its quiet, shady streets and tasteful dwellings reminding one of a New England village. But while it has long been an educational centre of the State, with several colleges and academies of high repute for the whites, it is in the very heart of what is known as the "black belt" of the Southern States, in the midst of a dense population not yet emerged from the shadows of slavery. Mr. Washington wrote in his first letter to his Hampton friends: "On Friday I rode about fourteen miles into the country to visit the closing exercises of one of the teachers. From this trip I got some idea of the colored people in the country. Never was I more surprised and moved than when I saw at one house two boys, thirteen or fourteen years old, perfectly nude. They seemed not to mind their condition in the least. Passing on from house to house, I saw many other children five and six years old in the same condition. It was very seldom that I saw any children decently dressed. If they wore clothing, it was only one garment and that so black and greasy that it did not look like cloth. As a rule, the colored people all through this section are very poor and ignorant, but the one encouraging thing about it is that they see their weakness and are desirous of improving. The colored teachers in this part of Alabama have had few advantages, many of them having never attended school themselves. They know nothing of the improved methods of teaching. They hail with joy the Normal School, and most of them will be among its students." And, on the whole, Mr. Washington concludes: "If there is one place in the world where a good Normal School is needed, it is right here. What an influence for good ; first on the teachers, and from them on the children and parents."

Before the week was over, thirty teachers had been enrolled as students, one of the colored churches opened its doors to the new enterprise, with a couple of neighboring shanties thrown in for recitation rooms, and the Tuskegee Normal School declared its independent existence on the Fourth of July, 1881.

The good will manifested toward the school by both white and colored was from the first a great encouragement. Mr. Washington wrote—quoting again his first letter—"I have had many kind words of encouragement from the whites, and have been well treated by them in every way. The trustees seem to be exceptional men. Whether I have met the colored people in their churches, societies, or homes, I have received their hearty co-operation, and a 'God bless you.' Colored preachers too seem to be highly in favor of the work, and one of the pastors here, fifty years old, is one of my students.'

The numbers rapidly increased, students coming from more distant parts of the State, and finding board in the town. On further request, Miss Olivia A. Davidson was recommended and appointed as Assistant Principal, another graduate of Hampton and afterwards of the Framingham Massachusetts Normal School. They employed a third Hampton graduate as assistant teacher. The Hampton trio held bravely on with work enough for all, but now a new difficulty presented itself.

Most of the students were without means to pay for even one full year's course. They had come with effort under the impulse of a new longing for improvement. They had found more profit than they had expected, and it was hard to give up. One after another, as their little stock was exhausted, came with tears in his eyes to Mr. Washington, to say: "My money is used up and I must go." Some, by cooking for themselves and living on little, tried to hold on through the year. Mr. Washington says: "I remembered the day I came to Hampton with but fifty cents in my pocket and she gave me a chance to help myself." Oh that it were possible—could it be possible to give such a chance to these?

While this question—hardly more than a wish—was rising in the hearts of the Hampton workers, an old plantation was thrown upon the market at Tuskegee, on unusually low terms; a hundred acres of fairly good land at $500. $200 down, with a farmhouse and out buildings in tolerable repair. A bold idea took possession of the young Principal. He wrote to the Treasurer of Hampton Institute and asked if it would be practicable to lend two hundred dollars to plant a Hampton seed in Tuskegee. The answer came—"To lend you

Hampton School funds—no. To lend you mine at my own risk—yes, and here is my check; and God speed you."

This generous trust was not careless or misplaced. The advantage of the purchase was apparent and the Treasurer knew his man. The two hundred dollars clinched the bargain for the land, and within two months were back in their owner's hands. Before three more, Mr. Washington wrote to his generous friend:

Tuskegee, Dec. 18, 1881.

" Four months and a half ago, without a dollar of our own, we contracted to buy a farm of one hundred acres at a cost of $500, on which to permanently locate our school. To day, the last dollar has been paid." And how? The young people went to work in the South, and their story was told in the North. Over a hundred dollars was raised right in Tuskegee by the efforts of teachers and students, by an "entertainment," a fair, and subscriptions of both colored and white friends. While this effort was going on, they were pleasantly surprised by a gift of one hundred dollars from a Massachusetts lady, a liberal friend of Hampton, and by one from the vacation students of the Hampton School—those remaining through the summer to work and study in the night school to earn money to keep themselves through the course. Entering with hearty interest into Mr. Washington's efforts for their Alabama brothers, they raised, through concerts and otherwise, nearly one hundred dollars toward the enterprise. A friend in Connecticut who had been favorably impressed by his observation of Mr. Washington's work with the Indians, gave two hundred dollars and promised a hundred more for tools, seeds, etc. if the balance then due should be raised in Alabama by January; a condition more than fulfilled, as we have seen.

So the new departure was made. The farm was deeded to a board of trustees, whose names may be read on a page preceding this sketch. They include representative names of North and South, white and colored, with a majority of no sect. The preparatory class of the increasing school took possession of the old farm house, and as soon as the early Southern spring opened, the boys went to work with joyful hearts to put in their first crops of corn and cotton.

Faith and will and working power grow by exercise.

" As soon as the farm is equipped," wrote the Principal, " We expect to direct our energies toward getting up a school building by next term. The present buildings on the farm will be entirely insufficient to accommodate the school next term. We may seem to be planning much, but remembering that God helps those who help themselves, we will go forward."

How they went forward, appears from the report of the exercises held on March 30th, 1882, in combined celebration of the close of the school's first session, and the laying of the corner stone of a new frame building by Hon. Waddy Thompson, County Superintendent of Education. With eloquent words, he bade the workers God speed, trusting that their labors might prove a blessing to their race, while a colored pastor feelingly exclaimed, " I thank God for what I have witnessed to day—something I never saw before, nor did I ever expect to see it. I have seen one who but yesterday was one of our owners, to-day lay the corner stone of a building devoted to the education of my race. For such a change, let us all thank God !" The report stated: " During the year, one hundred and twelve students from various parts of the State have attended the school, and now during vacation, many of them are doing good work as teachers by which to earn money to return next year. By the aid of the people in Tuskegee in labor and money, and help from the Northern friends, the lumber is now on the ground, the building is being framed and we are making every effort to have it completed by the beginning of the next session, Sept. 1st, 1882."

At large meetings in New York and Brooklyn, convened that spring in the interest of Hampton Institute, the story of the "young Hampton" at Tuskegee was also told. Its Principal and Assistant Principal spent their summer vacation in the North in the cause, with all the introductions and encouragements that Hampton could give. October 15th, Miss Davidson wrote to the *Southern Workman* published by Hampton Institute: " As I wrote last spring, we had received for our school building, at the close of school, $1000. During the summer, I am glad to be able to tell you, we succeeded in raising the remainder necessary, in the North, so that the money for

the building is provided for. The work on it is being rapidly carried
forward and we hope to go into it the first of the coming month, a
great relief from our present very crowded quarters. School opened
the 4th of September with quite a full attendance, and now the number is more than double that of this time last year, and we have ap-
plications from many who desire to come in later. During the sum
mer, a number of our most advanced students taught school in this
and adjacent counties, and reports came to us from many of these
places, of the superior work done by these compared with that of
others who had not had the year's training."

Another pleasant result of the Normal School's influence is re-
corded in the same letter. "That the denominational spirit is very
strong here is shown by the fact that the colored public schools have
been taught for years as separate denominational schools, the Baptist children attending the Baptist, and the Methodist children, the
Methodist school. This year, however, we have gained the consent
of the people to the union of the two on our farm, as training school
for the Normal, under the care of two Hampton graduates. To-day,
for the first time here in many years; the children of the two denominations met in school together. This school will, when all are in,
number over three hundred, and the Normal School one hundred, so
that by Christmas we shall have on our farm in daily attendance of
public and Normal School students, perhaps more than four hundred.
When we realize what the work of these students is to be, how
necessary it is for them to be well fitted to go into this work with
earnestness and ability, and how far in the future their influence for
good or bad may extend, can we doubt the importance of the work
before us?"

The new building stands upon the site of the old farm house,
pleasantly shaded by ancient cedars, mulberries and magnolias, and
was named Porter Hall after one of its chief contributors. It is a
frame building, 67 x 58 ft. and three stories high without the basement; containing six recitation rooms, a large chapel, a reading room
and library, a boarding hall, and in the third story, dormitories for
girls. The young men continued to board in the town, working their

way, to some extent, on the school farm. The Principal and teach-
*ers rented a small cottage near the place, and the primary training
school occupied what had been the stables.

After moving into its new quarters, the school work went vigorously on through the winter, with 130 students, representing nearly
every part of the State, with some even from Georgia.

PORTER HALL.

And now came a new and great encouragement. In February,
1883, the State Legislature increased the appropriation for the school,
from two to three thousand dollars annually, on the recommendation

of the Superintendent of Public Instruction, Hon. H. Clay Armstrong.
The Committee on Education reported it unanimously to the House
and the Governor recommended its passage.   As some of the mem-
bers who were ignorant of the character of the school, raised objec-
tions to this increase at a time when, by defalcations of the State treasurer, reported only the day before, the State had lost a quarter of a
million, the Speaker of the House, Col. W. F. Foster, member from
Tuskegee, an ex-Confederate soldier, left the chair and in an eloquent and effective speech in praise of Mr. Washington and his work
urged its passage.   On his conclusion, the bill passed through all its
readings, by a nearly unanimous vote.   It promptly passed the Senate also, received the approbation of the Governor and became a law.
Mr. Washington was invited to make a statement of his work before
the committee of the Senate on education, and especial interest was
manifested in its industrial features.

About the same time, Mr. Washington was notified by the State
Supt. of Education, Hon. H. Clay Armstrong, that, on his recommendation, $500 had been awarded to the School from the Peabody fund.

In the letter announcing this good fortune to the *Southern
Workman*, Mr. Washington reports other pleasing encouragements,
external and internal, from friends North and South, and in the spirit of the school.

" We had a pleasant two-days' visit last month from Rev. R. C.
Bedford, of the American Missionary Association, pastor of the Congregational Church of Montgomery.   He spoke one evening to the
students and citizens in our chapel.   It was crowded and he seemed
to impart new life to everybody.   On Thanksgiving Day we had exercises in the chapel, and addresses were delivered to the students and
visitors by the pastors of the white Baptist and Presbyterian churches and by one of the colored pastors.   Thursday and Friday evenings
and on Saturday, Miss Davidson, assisted by the other teachers, held
a fair to raise means for the school.   All thought that at the fair, the
people showed in a practical way that they were willing to help themselves all they could.   We netted from the fair, $145. $45 of this
amount came from a " jug-breaking " Friday evening.   The jugs had

been given out a month previous to twelve students who left few persons unbegged for a nickel. /

Soon after we moved into the building, the young men were told that a large amount of earth would have to be removed from the basement before it could be completed, and if we had to hire it done, the cost would be $30 or $35. One young man suggested to the others, that since friends had been kind enough to pay the greater part needed to put up the building, students ought to be willing to give in work whatever they could. A proposal was made that they should be divided into squads and each squad work every day in turn for an hour after school. This was done willingly by all, and the basement was cleared out.

Within a few days, a kind friend from Connecticut has sent us means to purchase an additional forty acres to our farm, making in all 140 acres.

By invitation of Capt. Wilson, Supt. of Education of Bullock county, I go to hold a two days' Institute with the colored teachers of his county. I will try to send you an account of my trip."

With such encouragement and such spirit, growth was inevitable. The school could not stand still. Enlargement was but a question of time and a short time.

In his first letter from Tuskegee in '81, Mr. Washington had written: "An institution for the education of colored youth can be but a partial success without a boarding department. In it they can be taught those correct habits which they fail to get at home. Without this part of the training, they go out into the world with untrained intellects and their morals and bodies neglected. After the land is paid for, we hope to get a boarding department on foot as soon as possible."

In April, '83, the school enjoyed a pleasant visit from General J. F. B. Marshall, the honored Treasurer of the Hampton Institute, whose friendly hand had been the first to start the young enterprise on its way. His visit gave it new cheer. He wrote to the *Southern Workman* of the situation there: "The farm contains one hundred and forty acres, and the boys are at work clearing a field for sugar-cane which grows well here.   They also raise cotton and sweet potatoes, peaches, etc.   To enable them to train the students properly, they must have them board at the school.   The new building will furnish in its upper story dormitories for the girls, but they have no quarters for the young men, who are at present boarding round in the town at a great disadvantage both as to training and labor. A building is needed for the accommodation, of say one hundred young men, which Mr. Washington says will cost about $8000 if their labor can be made available in its construction.   For this purpose, he proposes to build of brick made on the farm which has excellent clay.   The young men are impatient to be set to work on their building : and as soon as money enough can be raised to pay the foreman, and start the brick-yard, it will be put in operation. The wood-lot is close to the clay, and fuel can be got for the hauling.   Two hundred dollars will secure a foreman long enough to make all the bricks needed for the building. As bricks are always in demand in the town which has no kiln, it would be a paying permanent industry. To finish the basement of the present building for a kitchen and dining room-$250 are needed. I hope the friends of Negro education and self-help will come forward and furnish Mr. Washington with funds to complete the work he has so well begun."

The next event in the history of the Tuskegee school was the celebration of its second anniversary, combined with the dedication of Porter Hall whose corner stone had been laid the year before. The dedication address was delivered by Rev. Geo. L. Chaney of Atlanta, formerly of Boston, one of the trustees of the school; and eloquent speeches were also made by Rev. Morgan Calloway, the associate in Emory College, of its President, Dr. Haygood, author of "Our Brother in Black," and by Rev. Mr. Owen, a colored pastor from Mobile. There was, as yet, no graduating class, but the students' recitations and drill and sweet singing added to the interest of the day which closed the second year of progress.

During the summer, a small frame cottage was put up with four rooms to hold sixteen young men, and three board shanties near the grounds were rented, roughly accommodating thirty six more.   In

September, a boarding department was opened for both sexes, and as many young men as could be provided for availed themselves gladly of the chance to work out half or nearly half of their board at the school. As soon as there is room for them, all non-residents of Tuskegee will be required to board at the school.

In September also, a pleasant surprise came to the workers in an unsolicited gift of $100, from the Slater Fund, and in November, the presentation of their needs to its efficient agent, Dr. Haygood, by their friend and trustee, Rev. R.C. Bedford, brought a response double their hopes, in an appropriation of $1000, for the equipment of their industrial department.

With this impetus, a carpenter shop was built and started, a wind mill set up to pump water into the school building, a sewing machine bought for the girls' industrial room, mules and wagons for the farm, and the farm manager's salary paid for nine months.

All through the summer, as through the previous one, the Principal and his associate had been earnestly presenting their cause at the North, with so much encouragement that the work on the new building was vigorously begun in the fall and winter. Mr. Washington could write triumphantly to the *Southern Workman* Feb. 15, 1884: "The new building which has now been begun will cost $10,000, and over $5,000 of this amount have been raised."

The extraordinary severity of the winter furnished its own spur to the work. Mr. Washington wrote Feb. 15th: "Not less than ten hands went up in the chapel a few nights ago, in answer to the inquiry how many of the young men had been frostbitten during the cold weather. The teachers were not surprised at this; on more than one night when making a tour of the rooms at a late hour to give a comforting word when there were no more blankets to give, have the young men been found hovering around the fire while the cold wind poured in through the roof, sides and floor of the room. While there has been this suffering, so anxious have the students been to remain in school that there has been almost no murmur of complaint. They have shown cheerfulness throughout. Must they be asked to endure the same another winter? We have faith to believe not. They want nothing done for them which they can do for themselves. They are now digging out the basement for the new building, and preparing the clay to begin moulding bricks as soon as the weather will permit."

In March, at public meetings held for Hampton Institute in Baltimore, Philadelphia, New York and Boston, the cause of the young Hampton also was again presented with marked success. In his forcible speech at these meetings, Mr. Washington was able to say: " Our young men have already made two kilns of bricks and will make all required for the needed building. From the first we have carried out the plan at Tuskegee of asking help for nothing that we could do for ourselves. Nothing has been bought that the students could produce. The boys have done the painting, made the bricks, the chairs, tables and desks, have built a stable and are now building a carpenter shop. The girls do the entire housekeeping, including the washing, ironing and mending of the boys' clothes. Besides, they make garments to sell and give some attention to flower gardening."

The new building, 43x76 feet and four stories high, is to be called Alabama Hall. On deliberation it was decided to devote this one to the girls' dormitories, with dining room, kitchen, laundry, parlor, reading room, and library for all the students and teachers, the young men then to occupy Porter Hall which will accommodate about one hundred.

The reconstructionary influence of the new effort has been strikingly shown already in its very beginnings. As Mr. Washington said in his speech : " Some of the country whites looked at first with disfavor on the establishing of this Normal School in Tuskegee. It turned out that there was no brick yard in the whole county. Farmers and merchants wanted to build, but bricks must be brought from a distance or they must wait for one house to burn down before building another. The Normal School, with student labor, started a brick yard. Two kilns of bricks were burned. The white people came from miles around for bricks. From examining bricks, they were led to examine the workings of the school. From a discussion of the brick yard came the discussion of the Negro's education ; and thus many of the "old masters" have been led to become interested in Negro education. Harmony will come in proportion as the black man gets something that the white man wants, whether it be of brains or material."

In a speech before the National Educational Association at Madison. Wis. this year, Mr. Washington said: "About one month ago, one of the white citizens of Tuskegee who had at first looked on the school in a cold, distant kind of a way, said to me: 'I have just been telling the white people that the Negroes are more interested in education than we and are making more sacrifice to educate themselves.' At the end of our first year's work, some of the whites said: 'We are glad that the Normal School is here because it draws people and makes labor plentiful' At the close of the second year, several said that the Normal School is beneficial because it increases trade, and at the close of the last session, more than one has said that the Normal School is a good institution: it is making the colored people in this State better citizens. From the opening of the school to the present,the white citizens of Tuskegee have been among its warm- . est friends. They have not only given of their money, but they are ever ready to suggest and devise plans to build up the institution. When the school was making an effort to start a brick-yard, but was without means, one of the merchants donated an outfit of tools. Every white minister in the town has visited the school and given encouraging remarks. The President of the white college in Tuskegee makes a special effort to furnish our young men work that they may be able to remain ir school.

A former owner of 75 or 100 slaves and now a large planter and merchant said to me a few days ago: 'I can see every day the change that is coming. I have on one of my plantations, a colored man who can read and write and he is the most valuable man on the place. In the first place, I can trust him to keep the time of the others or with anything else. If a new style of plow or cotton planter is taken on the place, he can understand its construction in half the time that any of the others can.' "

In April, the school had the pleasure of a visit from the Lady Principal of Hampton Institute, an extract from whose letter to Hampton from Tuskegee will be found in another part of this pamphlet.

In May, the first number was issued of " *The Southern Letter, Devoted to the education of the head, hand and heart. To be published monthly by the Tuskegee Normal School. Booker T. Washington, editor, Warren Logan, business manager.*" This little sheet, at present 9 x 12, will undoubtedly grow, and a good way to encourage the industrial and educational work at Tuskegee will be to send the 50 cents for its year's subscription. Its first number contained the pleasant news that to the hundred acres of land with which the school started, its Connecticut friend had added an adjoining tract of 480 acres of farming and wood land; and that, by the gift of a job printing press through a Boston lady, card and bill head printing had been added to the industries of Tuskegee.

The June number of the *Southern Letter* contained a report of the third anniversary of the Normal school, on May 29. 1884. Many visitors were present, white and colored. The great interest was in the development of the department of industrial training which now included besides the farm, the Slater carpenter shop and blacksmith shop. the printing office, the girls' industrial room, and the brick yard, where the students were making brick for Alabama Hall. The morning exercises were as usual, inspection, recitations and review of the current news, and the speaker of the afternoon was Prof. R. T. Greener, of Washington, who delivered a very practical and eloquent address. Reporters were present from Montgomery and Tuskegee, and an extract from the report of the Tuskegee *Weekly News*, the white democratic paper of the place, will be found among the outside testimony on another page of this pamphlet.

The school then broke up for its summer work. About fifty of its students are teaching this vacation; fifteen remain to work on the farm, at the brick yard and on Alabama Hall during the summer, and attend night school. Nine of them have been attending night school and working all day, through the past term, to earn money to keep themselves in the day classes next year.

It is evident that this well *lettered* Institution has not only added to its course in the three R's, as Miss Davidson's bright letter claims, "the three C's—cotton, corn and cane"—but teaches also the three P's— Providence, Pluck and Progress.

BUILDINGS IN WHICH THE SCHOOL WAS STARTED.

The Principal and his associates are doing their part again to de-monstrate their faith in them. The new move for this summer's cam-paign is the sending out by the school of a quartette of singers, three of them its students and one a teacher, to sing at the various summer resorts in New England and the Middle States. Their object is to raise the $4000 now required for the completion of Alabama Hall. Mr. R. H. Hamilton, who has had much experience with the well known "Hampton Singers," has kindly consented to lead them. They will also be accompanied by the Principal. The young men compos-ing the company of singers, having no money to give for the work at Tuskegee, freely give their services and their songs during the sum-mer. They will sing the "plantation songs" as they hear their parents sing them in Alabama, without any polish. It is hoped that they will sing their way to the hearts and the help of the people.

The story of Tuskegee is not finished, but having brought it down to the present moment, we look to the friends of general education and self-help for the next chapter.

LIFE IN AND AROUND THE SCHOOL.

FROM A TEACHER'S STANDPOINT.

BY WARREN LOGAN.

HOW IT PAYS.

It is sometimes asked, Does it pay to educate the Negro? Well, that depends, for him as for others, upon how he is educated.

An old colored man in a cotton field in the middle of July, lifted his eyes toward heaven and said : "De cotton is so grassy, de work is so hard, an' de sun am so hot, dat I believe dis darkey am called to preach."

There is no doubt that some of the would be teachers, as well as the would be preachers, in their desire for education are inspired, as some of their brothers in white are, by a yearning not for usefulness but for ease. Simply to gratify them in this would certainly not pay for generous contributions to their education.

But if along with mental training, the Negro is taught that, as President Garfield told the students at Hampton Institute, "Labor must *be*, and labor must be free;" that in free labor is dignity and prosperity and self-respect; if with his book learning, he learns to respect the rights of others, to do right from a love of right, and is given some useful trade for his start in life, why will it not pay handsomely to educate him ; to make him an intelligent and useful American citizen instead of an ignorant and dangerous one ?

This is the work of the industrial school. This is the work of Tuskegee, the very place for our cotton field candidates.

The great need of the South is competent school teachers and skilled mechanics. The demand for both is much greater than the supply. Colored lawyers might perhaps be dispensed with for a while, but colored teachers, able to use both head and hands, are an actual, present necessity.

Tne great majority of our Tuskegee students hope to become teachers among their people. Almost all of them come from the country, and are good material. Visitors are struck with their splendid physical proportions. Most of them are stalwart, robust young people, well able to work their way in the world and eager for the opportunity. They have had poor home training, and it is necessary to teach them correct habits of living, but they evince an eagerness to learn that is as surprising as it is encouraging, undergoing, in many instances, much privation and discomfort to keep in school. It is gratifying to watch the change that gradually takes place in their personal appearance, in clothes and manners, and expression of face.

The avidity with which they take hold of their studies is in striking contrast with the indifference and even repugnance to textbooks we hear of as common in white schools. The novelty of learning, to the Negro, gives it an attractiveness which is a potent stimulus to mental effort. The girls, who number nearly half the school, organized last term a "reading and talking club," in which they read and talk about those things that tend to refine their manners and brighten their minds. The boys have their debating societies, which are of some profit as well as fun. The disposition to improve themselves is encouraged by the teachers, who supply them, as far as is in their power, with good reading matter, and direct their efforts. Talks on the topics of the day are given often, and they are daily informed and examined on the current news.

The course of study as planned, extends through four years, but few can complete it without staying out for as much as a year to earn money. We do not think they will lose by this in the end. We hope to graduate our first class next year. The course is thorough in English lessons, composition and reading, with studies in literature. It extends in mathematics through elementary geometry, and includes geography, history, civil government with special study of the school laws of Alabama, book keeping, some study of the natural sciences, mental and moral philosophy, free hand drawing, vocal music, and the methods and practice of teaching. In the model school connected with the Normal, two regular teachers are employed, under whom our students practice as teachers.

As an industrial school, Tuskegee regards its manual labor depart-ment not merely as a means to secure education, but as a valuable part of education. Work is required of all. The boys are taught practical farming, carpentry, printing, brick making, black-smithing and painting; the girls, sewing and house keeping. The school hopes to add other industries as it becomes able.

We do not find that the manual labor system interferes seriously with the studies. We believe that in the long run, it will be found far more of a help than a hindrance, through its influence upon character and habits of industry. Of course, it makes a busy day for students and teachers, from the rising bell at half past five, and the work bell calling some after breakfast to their work shops or cotton fields and others to the fresh morning study hour, to the bell for "lights out" at half past nine at night, when the sleep of the laborer is sweet. A busy day, but Tuskegee has work to do and means to do it.

LETTERS FROM STUDENTS.

The following letters, written by students to friends, and published by permission in the *Southern Letter*, give an idea of what the school is doing for the students and of what they, in turn, are doing for themselves and their people :

A NIGHT STUDENT.

Tuskegee, Ala., May 12, 1884.

Dear S—: I have made up my mind to educate myself. I am now working at the brick-yard. I am working in the day and attending school at night. In this way I am learning and making money too. The school pays me so much a month for my work. I expect to work hard and save money, to go in the day school next term. We have a good teacher in the night school. I do not expect to come home inside of three months.

Your brother,

A. J. WOOD.

TEACHING AND PLOWING.

Tuskegee, Ala., May 14, 1884.

Dear Friend:

I am now in school in Tuskegee. I commenced in 1881. I have had the luck to return to school every fall since then, soon after the opening of the school. But be assured that it took and now takes hard work on my part to do this. My school in vacation paid only $18.00 per month. On Saturdays I plowed for Mr. James Johnson and he allowed me from 50 to 60 cents per day. Sometimes I would not take the money, but would take meat and meal. In this way I managed to board myself. I have been doing this way every vacation since 1881, and by so doing I keep myself in school.

I would not have been so hard pressed in money matters, but the first year I came to school I had to borrow money to carry me through, for I had loaned all I had before coming. This money I had to return when I opened my school after leaving school. So you see what circumstances I was put into. I have a chance to work out a part of my expenses while in school.

I am expecting to teach in Pike county this summer near Troy, Ala. I am informed that the school will not pay much, so I am going to do there as I did in Russell, that is, teach during school-days and work Saturdays.

Mr. R. B. Ballard is going to assist me in getting some work to do on Saturday. I am not ashamed to put my hand to any kind of honest labor. I see a blessing and beauty in it. I am trying to obtain an education that I may be able to go out into the world and do good for others. Yours truly,

L. D. McCullough.

A STUDENT'S VACATION WORK.

Society Hill, Ala.

Dear Miss D.:

I will tell you about my school during vacation.

On the 8th of June, 1883, I opened school on Forberst's Plantation, five miles from Society Hill, in Macon County, Ala. The people that lived on this plantation were thickly settled. They numbered one hundred and twenty, children and all. I found them very ignorant. They knew little about Sunday school. Some of them had never left the plantation since their birth.

The first day that I opened, fifteen pupils attended. My number increased daily. The school house was made of logs ; and it was covered and ceiled with boards. The roof was flat. The rain instead of running off would pour in. It had no ventilation except the door. Most of the boards were pulled off to let the air in through the big cracks. My pupils increased to eighty-five. When I had about fifty I could scarcely find a place to stand. To remedy this, I requested the patrons to build me a bush arbor : for the school room was not as large as a good sized bed room. The arbor was attached to the western end of the house. It was covered with bushes, which were cut and dragged by the boys. The seats were made under the arbor, also in the room. of pieces of unplaned plank laid across something like a stool.

I employed a lady teacher to assist me. She taught under the arbor. I would send out two classes at a time. I found this to be very pleasant except when it rained. When this occurred I would send the children to my boarding room for recitation. This was about fifteen yards from the arbor. The children delighted in passing backwards and forwards. It was some trouble to keep them quiet while passing. I taught on this plantation three months. My scholars learned very fast. They were obedient. It was seldom I ever used the rod. The patrons would visit the school every Friday evening to hear the children speak and sing. At the close of the school we had a big dinner, singing, speaking, acting, dialogues, &c., in the afternoon. My closing exercises were in the second story of a very large gin house. At the expiration of the three months the children and patrons had improved very much. I also had a nice Sunday school. Old and young attended. To elevate the people as much as I could, I would go up in the *quarter* every evening after school and spend some time in reading and talking to the old people. I would teach the girls how to make trimmings. Respectfully.

JOSIE A. CALHOUN.

HELPING ONE'S SELF.

I decided some time ago to educate myself in some way or other. I had several ways before me. Out of these I expected to obtain the means to keep me in school. I thought that I would teach school some. and go to school some. This failed to keep me just as I wanted to; yet I desired to continue in school. Another was to ask help of my friends. I found that they didn't mean to be friends in a way like that. I looked about and found my aims still unfinished. When

I saw that I could not get help in this most needy time. I thought of a fable that I once read.

A bird had built its nest in a farmer's cornfield—it was near the time of harvest. She said to her young each day she left them, to listen to what you hear the farmer say. They did so, and delivered the message to her as soon as she returned. She said to them, you need not be afraid so long as he depends upon his neighbors : but when you hear him say he will reap the corn himself, then we had better be gone, for the work will be done. So it was with my friends. Now I have decided to help myself.

I find this the only successful way.

R. T. WELLBORN.

———

KEEPING HIMSELF IN SCHOOL BY DOING HIS OWN COOKING AND WASHING, AND CUTTING CORD WOOD.

The following letter is from a young man who entered school when it was organized, and, although he then had a family, he has not remained out of his classes two whole months at a time during the three years. He has supported his family and walked a distance to and fro of 25 miles every week to see and assist his family.

Dear friend:

When the Tuskegee Normal School opened for the purpose of training colored teachers for Public Schools of this State, I made up my mind to complete a normal course for that especial purpose. I entered school July 4th, 1881. After buying my books, I did not have enough money to pay for a month's board. I thought the best way to make a little money go a long ways would be to hire my cooking done and pay house rent. Six of us young men hired the lady of the house to do our cooking, each paying a dollar a month. By being business manager for the lady, I made one dollar pay for two and a half months.

A little later a friend told me that he would let me have a room free of charge and I could do my cooking. My money being out, I accepted the offer gladly. When I did not go home to my family, I did my own washing.

During the vacation of our school, I taught school in Pike County
Ala., in the summer of 1882. I received eighty eight dollars for four
months teaching. I came home in the fall and settled all my debts,
and then entered school. Just before my school was out in Pike
County, I wrote to one of the trustees of the Normal School, telling
him that I would have to begin at once to work so that I might stay
in school when I entered, because it would take all my money to pay
my debts and to buy the required number of books.

He got a place for me at Mr. James Alexander's, where I could pay
house rent by chopping wood and drawing water. I was paid extra for
working in the garden and currying the horse. When school vacated
in the summer of 1883, I went home to work on the farm that my wife
was carrying on. Not making enough money to pay board in school,
I returned to Mr. Alexander's, in the fall of 1883, on the same terms
which have been mentioned. During the fall of 1883, I cut wood nearly every evening and Saturdays and sometimes on Mondays; I cut in
all forty eight cords of wood at forty cents a cord.

Being a poor boy, I always manifested a great interest in whatever
I did for those who hired me, and numbers of times persons would
pay me more than they agreed to pay at first.

Yours,

J. T. HOLLIS.

Cotton Valley, Macon Co., Ala., June 5th, 1884.

BOYS' QUARTERS.

A NEW VIEW OF THE CIVIL RIGHTS BILL.

The classes, beginning with the first in the order of their advancement, are required to give items of current news each morning. This requirement is profitable in teaching the students to read newspapers and in broadening their ideas. Occasionally some very ludicrous things are developed in the course of the exercise.

A case in point. Shortly after the decision of the Supreme Court setting aside the Civil Rights Bill was made, a boy on being asked to explain the nature of the bill just declared unconstitutional, arose in his seat and very innocently said, "It was a bill introduced for the civilization of the Members of Congress"

FATHER PERRY.

There is a church near Tuskegee which has a total membership of two hundred, and nineteen of these are preachers. Now, as before the war, there are a great number of unordained, irregular ministers among the colored people, mysteriously termed, with some implied disrespect of their irregularity, "jackleg preachers" ; licensed then by their master's will, now by their ability to attract a congregation ; "called" by some Macedonian vision, or perhaps by the desire to help themselves to a living in an easy way. Ignorant of books and systems, they understood thoroughly the art of winning the sympathies of their hearers and of firing them with their own fervid enthusiasm. With their advancement in other directions, the Negroes have advanced in the intelligence and propriety of their modes of worship and the demand for an educated ministry. It will be well however if this one art of the old time preachers is not forgotten.

Elder Thomas Perry—Father Perry, as he is familiarly called in

Tuskegee where he still preaches as an evangelist though nearly eighty years of age—is an interesting representative of the old time preachers who are fast passing away. He is no "jackleg preacher," but one who has borne the burden and heat of the day, in bondage and freedom, and by the purity and piety of his life and his devotion to his people's good, has won the respect and affection of a large circle of friends in both races.

On a recent visit to his modest home, he was persuaded to give to some of the teachers from the Normal School some memories of his long life, interspersed now and then with a free expression of his opinions which are quite decided, like his character.

"I was born," said Father Perry, "in Hancock Co. Ga. about 1805, as near as I can tell. But I have lived in five different counties in Georgia, two in Alabama and one in Mississippi. I learned to read by toting my spelling book in my hand while plowing. I had no teacher but a little colored boy that I used to mate with. His young master had taught him."

"What reader did you use?"

"If any, I dont remember. I did use the Testament a little—only by chances. now and then."

"About how old were you when you thought of preaching?"

"I reckon I was about twenty-five."

"Had you any encouragement from others to preach?"

" Nothing that could be called encouragement. We went pretty much altogether on our own hooks in those days."

"Suppose you give us a general sketch of your life."

"I'm too old to remember all particularly. but I'll do the best I can. '

I began to preach in Harris County Georgia. I had no difficulty in getting the people together to hear me. I respected other people and noticed how respectable people act. That was how I won them.

I never had any great difficulty in getting along. I have never been drunk in my life. I haven't done so well since the surrender as I did before. I have always had a large congregation wherever I have been. I believe I did greater work before the war than I have

done since. I was moved to preach simply by a sense of duty to
help my people in the salvation of their souls. I met with no opposition from white or colored. Many of the slave people professed
Christ in our revivals. I was in with the white church and always
had free access to the people.

Most of my life, I have had charge of some church. I am now
what they call an evangelist. Since the war I have been successful
as a minister if I understand what the mission of a minister is. I
understand that to be to convict sinners of their sins, and lead them
to Christ, and so to talk to those who are already professors of the
faith that they may be strengthened in their efforts to continue in the
straight road.

In getting up revivals, I have always first worked on myself; then
I would aim at the hearts of the Christians. If they didn't become
warm in the time I had calculated on, I continued any how. I always
tried to keep them from seeing any giving up on my part. During
slavery, I was in revivals with white people quite frequently. Since
the war, I have been in a revival every year. I don't like the way
many camp meetings are carried on. I think they can be so conducted
as to be of harm. I don't believe in selling on the camp grounds. It
is a hindrance to the religious influence. The people visit the stands.
They should be where the preaching is.

On starting out to preach, and on finding out my deficiencies, I
looked wholly to God. I determined from the first to learn what I
could about the Scriptures, but I did not see at first how deficient I
was ; that knowledge came gradually. I have paid some attention to
the newspapers, but very little. I have confined my study mostly to
the Bible and references to it. I have learned a great deal too by ar-
gument and conversation with fellow laborers in the ministry. At the
start, I firmly decided to say nothing in any assembly without a good
motive. I don't believe in studied oratory in a preacher. I don't
believe that is generally successful in getting up a revival. There
is an inward feeling that it is contrary to the apostles' practice. There
is a way, and there is something that is no way. Any thing that interferes with the working of the Holy Ghost is harmful. This is the

way I have always settled that question. I am also opposed to any extreme in what we call the *natural* way of preaching. I have been very much given to reproving my people. I have felt it my duty to do so. I think our young men should strip themselves of earth and preach the gospel. If there is no change, the people will all go wrong. My great desire is for my race to be united. I have always opposed having so many denominations among our race. There is too much opposition among us at this period of our growth. I have also found it injurious to religious work to have so many churches a mile or two apart.

My life was spent before the war mostly in farming for the whites. I rented a farm after the war with another man. He failed, so it all fell on me. I wasn't able to meet it all, so I failed too. I haven't been sick in bed a day for forty years."

FATHER PERRY. 82 YEARS OLD.

THE SHANTY SCHOOL AND CABIN HOME.

All the while the farm was being paid for, we were going daily to school in the old church and shanty. The latter was at least well ventilated. There was one thickness of boards above and around us, and this was full of large cracks. Part of the windows had no sashes and were closed with rough wooden shutters that opened upward by leathern hinges. Other windows had sashes but little glass in them. Through all these openings the hot sun or cold wind and rain came pouring in upon us. Many a time, a storm would leave scarcely a dry spot in either of the two rooms into which the shanty was divided to make room for separate classes. These divisions were small, but into them, large classes of thirty or forty had to be crowded for recitations.

But if the discomforts of the school room were great, many of the students had even greater ones in their home life. The colored people of Tuskegee generally are poor, and have few of the commonest comforts of life. Some of their houses are miserable hovels, letting in the cold and rain even more freely than do our school shanties. In rainy seasons, the students, after sitting all day in damp clothes and wet school room, had to go at night to boarding places where these and other discomforts were multiplied. In spite of all these disadvantages, they pursued their studies with cheerfulness and earnestness. Some indeed seemed scarcely to realize that they needed anything better, but it was felt by us who had the work in charge that much more ought to be done towards teaching them to live better lives in every way, than could possibly be done as they were situated. We could not reach them surrounded constantly as they were by influences in every way the opposite of elevating. We felt this especially for the girls. They were scattered about over the town in boarding houses, some of which our judgment condemned, while we could see them only for the few hours of the day when all were busy with recitations. Our most pressing need was a building into which we could gather both our girls and our boys, not only for school teaching but home teaching, for homes are what our people need.

JOHNSON'S "KYARRIAGE."

In Alabama, very few of the colored people have acquired homes of their own ; the majority are still living on lands owned by former masters. Immediately after the abolition of slavery, all were filled with the brightest anticipations of what freedom was to bring them. But here, as in some other parts of the South, the mortgage system of paying rent is common, and has conquered the freedman, in spite of his struggles.

Ten years ago, if you talked to one of these farmers, he had bright visions of the future to tell you. He was in the midst of troubles he does not now meet, but, as his song went, " 'T would be better furder on." Talk to him now, and you are struck by the entire want of hopeful expressions. Year after year of hard but vain toil has crushed all hope out of him, and he has settled stolidly down to his fate of getting barely sufficient rations to keep soul and body together, paying his rent and *clearing* at the end of the year a large debt with which to begin the new one.

The fact that few of these colored farmers under the mortgage system ever come out ahead, is due to more causes than one, and perhaps one of the main causes is their own mismanagement ; but the fact remains, and t'is the fact that has discouraged them. To one idea, however, the freedman has clung, through all his hardships and failures. That is the idea of education, if not for himself, for his children. It is through this feeling almost entirely that this people must be reached and helped.

The minister of a colored Baptist church in Tuskegee said to me recently ; "Ah, I tells yer, dis yere freedom aint what we culie'd ones t'ought it ud be afore it comed.

I t'ought when I was sot free, I'd soon hab a fine hoss, an' a kyarriage an' sarvents to drive me roun'! But Johnson's ben a' work-in' ebber sence de s'render, an' he aint got no fine hoss an kyarriage yet. He got one ole mule an' a wagon, an' dey all he spec's to git to kyarry him roun'. Ef he kin on'y git togedder 'nuff to feed an' clothe him, an' sen' his chillens to school, its all he spec's to git." "But," he added with earnestness! "I tanks God I's free to hab all dat "

Education is the freedman's carriage, and with the team of will and work,—with some charitable oiling of the wheels—it will carry his children up the steep hill before them.

EXTRACTS FROM "SOUTHERN LETTER."

Published Monthly by the Tuskegee Normal School.

B. T. WASHINGTON, Editor.

WARREN LOGAN, Business Manager.

At least fifty of our students will teach in the public schools of the State during the summer.

A blacksmith shop is now being built by the students.

Nine young men are learning the carpenter's trade.

Young men and young women, life is before you. It is in your power to choose *now* whether you will all through life be the slave of ignorance or a complete man or woman developed as God meant you to be.

Our population numbers 50,000 000, and one eighth, or 6,240 000 over the age of ten years, are illiterate. Assigned geographically, in the North there are 1,340,000 illiterate whites and 156,000 illiterate Negroes ; in the South, 1,676,000 illiterate whites and 3,064,000 illiterate Negroes.

The Model School closed with an interesting exhibition on Tuesday night, May 27. A large number of parents and visitors were present.

The annual meeting of the Alabama State Teachers' Association took place at the Tuskegee Normal School building on April 19th, continuing two days. The leading institutions and public schools of the State were represented, and the attendance was large and interesting.

Alabama is paying $9000 annually towards the support of colored normal schools. There are three in the State. Tuskegee is the only industrial school.

We keep three points in view: First, to give the best mental training; second, to furnish the student labor that will be valuable to the school and that will enable the student to learn something from the work within itself; third, to teach the dignity of labor.

The work department well systematized can be carried on with almost no loss to the student in his classes.

"We see now why reconstruction failed. Not because the constituency was black but because the mass was ignorant, and no community, black or white, can safely sit by and submit to be ruled by ignorant suffrage."—*Prof. K. T. Greener.*

An interesting feature of the industrial work on Anniversary day at Tuskegee this year was a general exhibit of industries in the library where, arranged in attractive order, were a rustic chair, a neatly made table and wash-stand from the Slater carpenter shop; bricks from the brick yard ; samples of oats, beans, potatoes, onions, collards etc., from the farm ; dresses, shirts, trimmings, crocheted mats and shawls, etc., from the girls' Industrial Room ; maps drawn by geography classes, geometrical figures, by the geometry class; herbariums from the botany class, and compositions, etc., from the grammar and rhetoric classes.

Our carpenter, assisted by several students, is getting out the window and door facings for Alabama Hall. The work is being done in the Slater carpenter shop.

Ground has been broken for Alabama Hall, and $6,000 of the $10,000 which it is to cost has been raised. We have faith to believe that our friends will give the remaining $4,000.

THE SCHOOL BRICKYARD.

OUTSIDE TESTIMONY.

A few extracts from letters and reports of Northern and Southern visitors of the Tuskegee Normal School, give testimony to the favor with which it is regarded by those who have been there or are familiar with its workings.

FROM A LETTER OF GEN. J. F. B. MARSHALL,

Treasurer of the Hampton Normal and Agricultural Institute, Hampton, Va.

To Southern Workman of May, 1883.

"A few day's rest from office duties being enjoined upon me recently, I determined to pay a visit to the Tuskegee School, in which the faculty and teachers of Hampton Institute naturally feel a special interest.

Tuskegee is one of the very old towns of the State, an attractive place of about twenty-five hundred inhabitants, having several colleges and academies of high repute for the white youth of both sexes. I was glad to find a very strong temperance sentiment here. There were only two bars in town and they pay a license of about nine hundred dollars each. No better location could have been chosen.

The leading white citizens of the place appreciate the importance of Mr. Washington's work and speak of him in high terms. He has evidently won the the esteem and confidence of all. Mr Foster, the present speaker of the House, in the State Legislature, lives here, and rendered valuable aid in getting the increased appropriation of the State for Mr. Washington of whom he spoke to me in high praise.

I am reminded by everything I see here of our own beginnings and methods at Hampton. I found on my arrival at the school, which is about a mile from the village centre, a handsome frame building of two stories and a mansard roof. Though not yet finished, it is occupied as a school building and is very conveniently planned for the purpose, reminding me of the Academic Hall at Hampton. The primary school on the Normal school grounds bears the same relation to it, as a practice school, that the Butler does to the Hampton Institute. It has 250 children on the roll. They are stowed away in what was the stable, close as crayons in a Waltham box. Let us hope they will all make their mark.

All six teachers of the Normal and training schools are colored; and to their race belongs all the credit of the work accomplished here and of the judicious use of the funds which the friends of the school through the efforts of Mr. Washington and Miss Davidson, have contributed.

The experiment, thus far so successful, is one of deep interest to all who have the welfare of the race at heart and should not be suffered to fail for want of means for its completion. It is vital to the success of this school that the students should all be brought under the training and supervision of the teachers by being boarded and lodged on the premises. Our experience at Hampton has shown the necessity of this. I know of no more worthy object or one conducive to more important results than this school enterprise, and I trust the friends of Negro advancement and education will not suffer it to languish or be hampered for funds. They may rest assured that these will be wisely expended and most worthily bestowed.

My three days' visit to Tuskegee was eminently satisfactory and has inspired me with new hope for the future of the race."

———

FROM THE LADY PRINCIPAL OF HAMPTON INSTITUTE.

May, 1884.

"The wish constantly on my my lips or in my heart, since I reached here last evening is that you could see this school. I am sure you would feel, as I do, that the dial of time must have turned back twelve years in its course. In many respects it is more like the Hampton I first knew than the one of to-day is; I was particularly struck by the plantation melodies which Mr. Washington called for at the close of the evening prayers; there is more of the real wail in their music

BARNS, BUILT BY STUDENTS.

than I ever heard elsewhere. The teachers here laugh over
their exact imitation of the *alma mater*; even the night school feature has sprouted; to be sure it only numbers two students, but it is on
the same plan as ours. Do you know that Mr.——has lately given
them 440 acres of land, making their farm now 580 acres?"

FROM REV. R. C. BEDFORD,

*Of the American Missionary Association: pastor of Congregational church in Mont-
gomery, Ala.*

Montgomery, Ala, March 1st, 1884.

GEN. S. C. ARMSTRONG:

Dear Sir:

A short time ago I made a trip to Tuskegee, Ala. for the purpose
of visiting the State Normal School for colored people located there,
four of whose five teachers, together with the wife of the Principal,
were once pupils of yours at Hampton Institute. * * * I attended the session of the school for two days and was exceedingly pleased
with the enthusiastic spirit of both teachers and pupils. One of the
encouraging features of the school is the warm interest it has inspired in many of the leading white citizens of Tuskegee. Mr. G. W.
Campbell and Mr. Wm. B. Swanson are among the oldest and most
respected citizens of Macon County. They with Mr. Lewis Adams,
a prominent colored man, constitute the State Board of Commission-
ers for the School. Colonel Bowen, Mr. Varner, and Col. W. F.
Foster—speaker of the present Legislature—all citizens of Tuskegee
and familiar with the school, are among its warmest friends. A short
time ago, in conversation with Hon. H. Clay Armstrong, our State
Sup't. of Education, I learned that he was so much pleased with the
work of Mr. Washington and his associates as to recommend to the
Committee on Education to report a bill giving $1000 per year ad-
ditional to the school. I was present during the debate on the bill.
So interested was Col. Foster in its passage that he left the Speaker's
chair, and upon the floor of the House, in an eloquent and effective

speech, urged that it pass. He sat down, and at once, by a vote of 59 to 18, the bill passed ; and is now a law.

With this example before us, we need have no fear as to what the colored people can do if, like Mr. Washington and his associates and pupils, they will take hold to win."

FROM THE REPORT FOR 1881-82 OF HON. H. CLAY ARMSTRONG,

State Superintendent of Education of Alabama.

"The Normal Schools are each in a prospering condition and doing faithful and efficient work. I deem it a privilege as well as duty, to make special mention of the school located at Tuskegee.

Though only authorized by an Act of Assembly approved March 1st, 1881, the friends of the enterprise proceeded at once to organize the School and to solicit funds in its aid. They have already raised by subscription, independently of the State appropriation, the sum of $1,521.94, and have erected a structure imposing in appearance to which they can point with exultant pride. For special particulars concerning this and other schools, I would invite your attention to the full and comprehensive reports accompanying and made a part of the report."

FROM A SOUTHERN WHITE DEMOCRATIC JOURNAL,

THE TUSKEGEE WEEKLY NEWS.

From an article of a column and a half in its isssue of June 5, 1884.

"This institution was established by an act of the Legislature of Alabama approved March 1, 1881, and $2000 was appropriated out of the general school revenue set apart for the colored children. * *

* * The school has just closed its third session and the exercises last Thursday were interesting, reflecting credit upon teachers and pupils. * * The property is deeded to a board of trustees including G. W. Campbell, President, M. B. Swanson and Lewis

Adams, the two first being the leading and most successful business men and among the most influential citizens of the community ; the latter is an industrious, deserving, intelligent colored man, who has the respect of his own race and the confidence of the whites. * *

Prof. B. T. Washington, the Principal, seems fully alive to the education of his race, and he is modest and retiring in disposition, seemingly desirous of the good will and respect of the whites. His efforts have been toward a wholesome and beneficial education of the pupils under his care, and we believe he has the respect of the community. * * * * * * * * * * *

The School adds greatly to the trade of Tuskegee, and the prejudice that existed against it at first is fact disappearing, and when its object and designs come to be fully understood, such feelings will not exist at all. * * * * * * * * * *

The buildings are not yet ample for the accommodation of the school, and the friends of the cause of education and of the colored race can find no better or more deserving place for practical aid and encouragement to that end. Of all the schools for the education of the colored people in Alabama, the Tuskegee Normal School stands at the head, and this is due to the excellent management and sound judgment of the Principal, to whom cannot be accorded too much praise by his race."

— — —

FROM REV. PHILLIPS BROOKS, D. D.

233 Clarendon Street, Boston July 5, 1884.

Mr. B. T. Washington,

My Dear Sir :

I am very glad to repeat what I said the other day, that I have great confidence in the purposes and methods of your work, and I wish you all success in your efforts to secure for it support and sympathy.

Yours most sincerely,

PHILLIPS BROOKS.

FROM REV. GEO. B. SPAULDING, D. D.

Manchester, N. H. June 25, 1884.

The colored labor school offers the best solution of the race problem at the South. To help the students under Principal Washington in their effort to build a new school house will prove no little help to this great cause. I can testify to the great merits of Mr. Robert Hamilton as leader of the Hampton Singers. His concert will not fail to be a great enjoyment to all lovers of music—and the noble cause he represents will heighten the pleasure.

GEO. B. SPAULDING.

FROM REV. ALEXANDER McKENZIE, D. D.

Cambridge, Mass. June 26, 1884.

I am happy to commend Mr. Booker T. Washington as a trustworthy and capable man, who is doing an excellent work in the Normal School with which he is connected as Principal. He is worthy of confidence and esteem; this present effort to secure funds for the most important work in which he is engaged deserves the approval of all who are interested in the welfare of the colored people.

The music which will be furnished by Mr. Washington and his associates is well known to those who have visited Hampton, and every one of them will speak in its praise.

ALEXANDER McKENZIE.

FROM GEN. S. C. ARMSTRONG.

The Tuskegee Normal School in charge of Mr. Booker T. Washington with nine assistants, all colored, is, I believe, the best work of its kind in the country under Negro control, and is worthy to be compared with any for that race in the United States.

Situated in the black belt of Alabama, amidst a dense and degraded people, it gives them what they need most and what they need now : a training of the head, hand and heart ; with a view of diffusing, through its graduates, a like teaching among the ignorant masses of that region.

Its 530 acres of wooded and 50 of cultivated land, Porter Hall, costing $6,500, besides brick-yard, carpenter and blacksmith shops, all paid for; with 169 pupils of both sexes, average age 18 years, fifty of whom are teaching during the summer ; besides six thousand dollars already secured towards a much needed building for girls' domitories and other purposes, to cost $10,000,—make a most encouraging showing, and a foundation for larger things.

The annual State appropriation of $3000, is a practical endorsement by the whites of the State of great value and meaning ; the property is, however, in private hands.

I have known Mr. Washington for over eight years, and regard him as one of the foremost men of his race, its leader in Alabama, and deserving of encouragement from all

S. C. ARMSTRONG,

Principal Hampton Institute, Virginia.

FROM GEN. J. F. B. MARSHALL.

I heartily endorse all that General Armstrong has said about this school, and a recent visit to Tuskegee has only strengthened my confidence in the ability of Mr. Washington and Miss Davidson to carry on successfully the important work they have undertaken.

J. F. B. MARSHALL,

Treasurer and Asst. Principal, Hampton Institute.

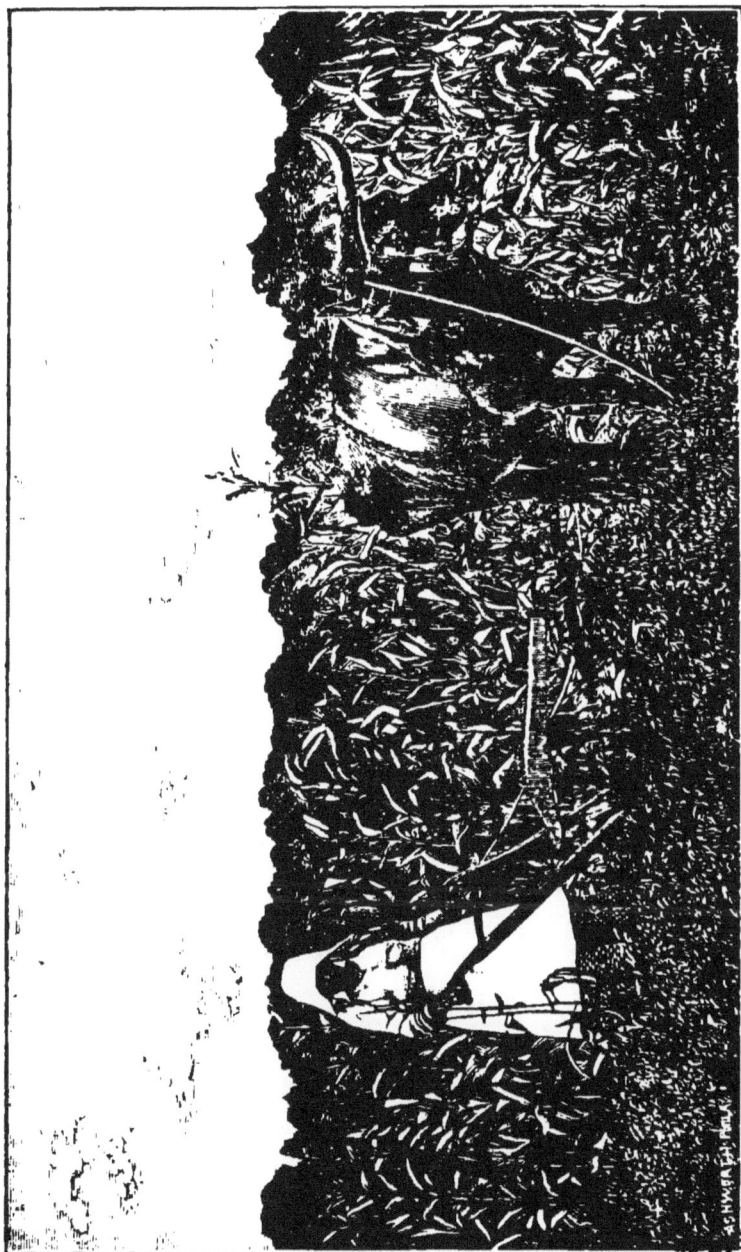

AUNT MARY, PLOWING.

CABIN

AND

PLANTATION SONGS,

AS SUNG BY THE

TUSKEGEE SINGERS.

ARRANGED BY

R. H. HAMILTON,

OF HAMPTON INSTITUTE, VA.

PREFACE TO MUSIC.

———

These songs have not, to our knowledge, been reduced to music before. We have endeavored to preserve the *melodies* as we heard them sung by the students at Tuskegee. They seem, in the main, to differ in character from those of the more northerly of the Southern States.

It is impossible to represent all the peculiar *turns* and *quavers* heard when these songs are sung by large gatherings of colored people in the South; and even if it were possible, it would be almost useless, for few musicians would be able to interpret them.

In reducing these melodies to writing, we have the double task of trying to preserve the original characteristics and at the same time make them intelligible through musical signs. The natural harmonies, as far as allowable, have been followed. Here and there effects have been introduced in the *harmony parts*, to assist in their rendition by so few voices. The great charm about many of the plantation melodies consists in the strength of the chorus and the "*vim*" with which they are sung.

We have added a few pieces of NEGRO MUSIC belonging to the period since emancipation, which we hope will prove none the less acceptable to purchasers of this book.

The words in these songs are common property. They are heard in all sections of the South, but set to different melodies. Many of the verses are irregular; familiarity with the melody and first verse will soon enable any one to adapt the others to the music.

R. H. HAMILTON.

Hampton, Va., July, 1884.

Fly to My Jesus' Arms.

SOLO. CHORUS.

1. Fly away, Be at rest, be at rest, be at rest, Fly away, Be at rest.

FINE. SOLO.

Fly to my Jesus' arms, Simon and Peter were fisher-men, Fished all night,

REFRAIN.

fish'd all day, Massa Jesus He came passing by, said, Drop your nets, Follow me,

D.C.

follow me, follow me, drop your nets, Follow me, fly to my Je-sus' arms.

2. Go down Gabriel and blow your horn.
 Go 'wake up nations, both great and small,
 Tell them I am coming now, going to
 Judge this world for action here, actions here, actions here,
 Judge this world for actions here.
 Fly to my Jesus' arms.—CHORUS.

3. When I was lying at hell's dark door,
 Never did lie so low before,
 Massa Jesus, He in passing by told me:
 Go in peace, sin no more, sin no more, sin no more.
 Go in peace sin no more.
 Fly to my Jesus' arms.—CHORUS.

I'm Going Home Children.

CHORUS.

I'm go-ing home, children, I'm go-ing home, children, I'm go-ing home, children, For the an-gels bid a me to come.

SOLO. **REFRAIN.**

One day as I was walking along, the angels bid a me to come. The el-e-ment opened and the love came down, For the angels bid a me to come.

2. Old Satan is mad and I am glad,
   The angels bid me to come,
   He missed that soul he thought he had,
   For the angels bid me to come.

3. As I went down in the valley for to pray,
   The angels bid me to come,
   When I got there, old Satan was there,
   For the angels bid me to come.

4. He said "you're too young to pray, too
        young to die,"
   The angels bid me to come.
   I made him out a liar and kept on my
        way,
   For the angels bid me to come.

5. Old Satan is a liar and a conjurer too,
   The angels bid me to come.
   If you don't mind he'll conjure you,
   For the angels bid me to come.

6. If you get to heaven before I do,
   The angels bid me to come.
Tell God's children I'm coming too,
   For the angels' bid me to come.

7. The tallest tree in Paradise.
   The angels bid me to come,
The Christian calls it the tree of life,
   For the angels bid me to come.

   * 8. Oh! hoist your flag children,
      Oh! hoist your flag children,
      Oh! hoist your flag children,
      For the angels bid me come.

* Sing last verse to the music of the Chorus.

He Locked the Lion's Jaw.

CHORUS.

Je - sus locked the li - on's, li - on's, Locked the li - on's li - on's,

Locked the li - on's, li - on's, Locked the li - on's jaw.   FINE.

1ST VOICE.

I'm a Meth - o - dist bred and a Meth - o - dist born, And

D.C.

when I'm dead, there's a Meth - o - dist gone.

2d VOICE.—I'm Catholic bred and Catholic born,
    And when I am dead there's a Catholic gone.—CHORUS.

3d VOICE.—I'm Baptist bred and Baptist born,
    And when I am dead there's a Baptist gone.—CHORUS.

4th VOICE.—I,m Presbyterian bred, I'm Presbyterian born,
    And when I am dead there's a Presbyterian gone.—CHORUS.

5th VOICE.—I'm Christian bred and Christian born,
    And when I'm dead there's a Christian gone.

The Hour is Come.

ANON.

SOLO. *Andante*

R. H. H.

1. To land in the harbor of darkness, The souls in the shackles of sin.
2. And we know as we go to meet Him, His bidding to do on the land,

Who bow to their idols in blindness, The gospel of Christ coming in.
As we walk o'er the water to greet Him, We feel the strong clasp of His hand.

For the vessels of God are all sailing, And the head light the dark waters o'er,
And tidings first sung by the angels, The "good will" that earthward they bore,

Is sending its gleam through the blackness, And Jesus still waits on the shore.
Shall encircle a world that shouts glory, To the Lord of the sea and the shore.

*The upper notes to be used for ending 2d Verse.

CHORUS. *Allegretto.* *rit.* *a tempo.*

The hour is come, the day draws near, We hear the coming car, Send forth the

glad tri-umphant cry, Hurrah! hurrah! hur-rah! From ev-'ry land by ev-'ry

sea, In shouts proclaim the great de-cree, All chains are burst, all

men are free, Hur-rah! hur-rah! hur-rah!

Toll the Bell.

CHORUS.

1 Go Ma - ry and toll the bell, Come John and call the roll, *M......

Slow. FINE. SOLO.

I thank God. 1. { Who's that yon - der, dress'd in black?
{ Who's that yon - der, dress'd in white?

REFRAIN. *Slow.*

Look like chil - dren just turn'd back, M...... I thank God.
Look like children of the Is - rael - ites, M...... I thank God.

2. Who is that yonder, dressed in blue?
Look like children just come through.
M............I thank God.
Who is that yonder dressed in red?
Look like children Moses led,
M............I thank God.—CHORUS.

3. Who is that yonder in the chariot ride,
Look like the Father and the Son at his side.
M............I thank God.
The Father has come with all His guest,
Going to judge this world from East to West,
M............I thank God.—CHORUS.

* Prolong the sound of M. with mouth closed.

Is there any Body Here Getting Ready to Die?

CHORUS.

1. Good Lord I wonder, Good Lord I wonder, Good Lord I wonder, Is there

FINE.

an - y bod - y here get - ting read - y to die.

1. You see them children dying ev'ry day, Is there any body here getting ready to die? You

D. C.

see them christians dying ev'ry day, Is there an-y bo-dy here getting ready to die?

2. You see them sinners dying every day,
   Is there any body here getting ready to die?
   Oh, judgment day is coming too,
   Is there any body here getting ready to die?

3. We hear poor sinners crying then,
   Is there any body here getting ready to die?
   Rocks, hills and mountains fall on me,
   Is there any body here getting ready to die?

4. The Saviour say depart from me,
   Is there any body here getting ready to die?
   Go down to hell that's prepared for you,
   Is there any body here getting ready to die?

The God of Elijah.

CHORUS

1. I be-lieve in the God of E-li-jah,— Oh,

yes! I be-lieve in the God of Dan-i-el,

Oh, yes! Do be-lieve, mem-bers, do be-lieve.

Oh, yes! Do be-lieve, mem-bers, do be-lieve,

FINE.

Oh, yes! 1. Some call me a Sun-day chris-tian

D.C.

Oh, yes! Some call me a Mon-day dev-il, Oh, yes!

2. Some call me a long-tongue liar,—Oh, yes!
But I will walk in the house of my Lord,—Oh, yes!

3. I will worship the God of Elijah,—Oh, yes!
I will worship the God of Daniel,—Oh, yes!

A Hymn.

B. T. T.

R. H. H.

1. And can it be, my soul, Thou hast for-got thy God, For-

got His end-less love t'ward thee, Or e'en for-got His rod?

2. Why shouldst thou choose the world,
Its fashion and its glare?
Thou seemest not my soul to know,
The world is but a snare.

3. Only in God who lives,
Canst thou e'er hope for peace;
Find only in His living word,
My soul, a sweet release.

Sound the Jubilee.

CHORUS.

Children, sound the ju-bi-lee. Children, sound the ju-bi-lee,

FINE.

Oh, children, sound the ju-bi-lee, Children, sound the ju-bi-lee!

SOLO.   REFRAIN.

1. I think I heard my Sa-viour say, I think I

heard my Sav-iour say, Sab-bath has no end, chris-tian,

Sab bath has no end, Oh, chris-tian,

D.C.

Sab-bath has no end, chris-tian, Sab-bath has no end.

2. ‖: Come my brother and go with me :‖
To that land above,
Believer to that land above,
Oh! believer to that land above,
Believer to that land above.

3. ‖: I think I heard my Saviour say, :‖
Ride in the chariot in the morn,
Seeker ride in the chariot in the morn,
Oh! seeker ride in the chariot in the morn,
Seeker ride in the chariot in the morn.

4. ‖: I think I heard my Saviour say, :‖
The fore wheels will run by faith,
Mourner the fore wheels run by faith,
Oh! mourner the fore wheels run by faith,
Mourner the fore wheels run by faith.

5. ‖: I think I heard my Saviour say, :‖
The hind wheels will run by grace,
Elder the hind wheels will run by grace.
Oh! elder the hind wheels will run by grace,
Elder the hind wheels will run by grace.

6. ‖: I think I heard my Saviour say, :‖
The inside's lined with gold;
Sister the inside's lined with gold,
Oh! sister the inside's lined with gold,
Sister the inside's lined with gold.

7. ‖: I think I heard my Saviour say, :‖
Walk the golden streets,
Preacher walk the golden streets,
Oh! preacher walk the golden streets,
Preacher walk the golden streets.

Faint Not.

Dr. B. T. Tanner.
Slow Chant.

R. H. Hamilton, 1882.

1. Faint not at e - ven tide, Ev - er hope on,
Je su is by my side, Though day be gone.

2.
What if the shades of night,
Do gather 'round,
Blinding thy keenest sight,
Darkness profound.

3.
What if upon the breeze,
Heavy with dews,
And from the shadowy trees,
Come sad curfews?

4.
Jesu is by thy side,
Ever hope on,
Soon will the eventide,
Likewise be gone.

Ode.

M. M. A K

R. H. H.

Rather slow.

1. We are stand-ing to-day in the sha-dow Of a part-ing soon to come, When our sad-dened hearts shall be riv-en, From our much loved Hamp-ton home.

Faster.

But the sun of hope is shin-ing

Be-yond the mounts of pain, And the fu-ture still is

rit.

smil-ing, Like vi-o-lets af-ter rain.

Like vi-o-lets.

2. We mourn not the past nor its struggles,
The Present our monarch reigns,
If we faithfully do his bidding,
Our future new triumph gains.
Then in fields lying white before us,
Where the laborers are few,
May our hands be strong and willing,
And our hearts be brave and true.

3. May the lessons which here we treasured,
In some spring-time yet to be,
Grow up and yield their harvest
That "the truth may make us free."
For the planting and tender training
Of the ivy that covers the rue,
For the courage and hope it gives us,
Alma Mater, thanks to you.

Love King Jesus.

REFRAIN.

1. Elder you say you love King Jesus, Elder you say you love the Lord. Lord. Oh,
come and let us know how you love King Jesus, Come and let us know how you love the Lord.

2. Sister you say you love King Jesus,
Sister you say you love the Lord.
REFRAIN.—Oh, shout and let us know how you love King Jesus,
Shout and let us know how you love the Lord.

3. Deacon you say you love King Jesus,
Deacon you say you love the Lord.
REFRAIN.—Oh, preach and let us know how you love King Jesus,
Preach and let us know how you love the Lord.

4. Brother you say you love King Jesus,
Brother you say you love the Lord.
REFRAIN.—Oh, pray and let us know how you love King Jesus,
Pray and let us know how you love the Lord.

5. Mourner you say you love King Jesus,
Mourner you say you love the Lord.
REFRAIN.—Oh, mourn and let us know how you love King Jesus,
Mourn and let us know how you love the Lord.

6. Children you say you love King Jesus,
Children you say you love the Lord.
REFRAIN.—Oh, sing and let us know how you love King Jesus,
Sing and let us know how you love the Lord.

Graduating Ode.

Miss M. A. Kensale.

R. H. H.

1. Alma Mater we ... thee, hope bright in our hearts, With gladness our work to pursue; Yet the sorrow of parting is

rit.

under our song. While we look toward the future with faith sure and strong, For we're

a tel.

going, dear Mater, from you.

FINE.

going.

2. But what-ever for us the future may hold. Success, failure, pleasure or pain; Thro'

m *f*

good and thro' ill thy hand we will grasp, And our zeal will grow stronger while

D.C.

feel - ing the clasp, And our hearts be en - couraged a - gain.

In My Heart.

CHORUS.

1. There's a bold little preacher in my heart, There's a bold lit - tle preacher in my

heart, In my heart, In my heart, There's a bold little preacher in my heart.

2. There's a little wheel turning in my heart,
   There's a little wheel turning in my heart,
   In my heart, in my heart,
   There's a little wheel turning in my heart,

3. I've a double 'termination in my heart,
   I've a double 'termination in my heart,
   In my heart, in my heart,
   I've a double 'termination in my heart,

4. I feel the spirit moving in my heart,
   I feel the spirit moving in my heart,
   In my heart, in my heart,
   I feel the spirit moving in my heart,

5. I feel like shouting in my heart,
   I feel like shouting in my heart,
   In my heart, in my heart,
   I feel like shouting in my heart,

Sister Mary's Twelve Blessings.

CHORUS.

1. El-der we will die in the field, Die in the field of bat-tle; Die in the field, Die in the field of bat-tle, Glo-ry in-a my soul. soul.

SOLO.

1. The ve-ry first blessing sis-ter Ma-ry had, It was the blessing of one, To think that her son Je-sus, Did go to work so young.
2. The ve-ry next blessing sis-ter Ma-ry had, It was the blessing of two, To think that her son Je-sus, Going to carry them mourners thro'.

D.C.

3. The very next blessing sister Mary had,
   It was the blessing of three.
   To think that her son Jesus,
   Going to set them prisoners free.

4. The very next blessing sister Mary had,
   It was the blessing of four,
   To think that her son Jesus,
   Going to preach among the poor.

5. The very next blessing sister Mary had,
   It was the blessing of five,
   To think that her son Jesus,
   Going to preach among the wise.

6. The very next blessing sister Mary had.
   It was the blessing of six,
   To think that her son Jesus,
   Is going to raise the sick.

7. The very next blessing sister Mary had.
   It was the blessing of seven,
   To think that her son Jesus,
   Had rose and gone to heaven.

8. The very next blessing sister Mary had.
   It was the blessing of eight,
   To think that her son Jesus,
   Going to open them pearly gates.

9. The very next blessing sister Mary had,
   It was the blessing of nine,
   To think that her son Jesus,
   Going to turn the water wine,

10. The very next blessing sister Mary had,
    It was the blessing of ten,
    To think that her son Jesus,
    Going to write without a pen.

11. The very next blessing sister Mary had.
    It was the blessing of eleven,
    To think that her son Jesus,
    Going to plead for us in heaven.

12. The very next blessing sister Mary had.
    It was the blessing of twelve,
    To think that her son Jesus,
    Had the keys of death and hell.

Oh, Stay in the Field!

CHORUS.

Oh, warriors.

1. Stay in the field, stay in the field, stay in the field, Un-

FINE.

til the war is ended. 1. When I was a mourner just like you, Until the war is

D.C.

ended, I never stopped till I come through, Until the war is ended.

2. I went to mourning all the day,
   Until the war is ended,
   Evening came and I went to pray,
   Until the war is ended.—CHORUS.

2. My eyes are turned to the heavenly gate,
   Until the war is ended,
   I'll keep on my way ere I be too late,
   Until the war is ended.—CHORUS.

4. The green tree's burning and why not the dry,
   Until the war is ended,
   My Saviour died and why not I.
   Until the war is ended.--CHORUS.

The Old Ark.

CHORUS.

Oh, the old ark's a mov-ing, move a-long chil-dren, The

old ark's a mov-ing, move a long home. home. 1. When Je-sus Christ con-

vert-ed my soul, In a my soul was a lit-tle white stone.

On that stone was a new-ly written, None could read it but those received it, I received it and I could read it; Just let me tell you what the stone

D. C.

did say, Redeemed, redeemed a been Son of God, Been washed in the blood of the Lamb.

2. When I was lying at hell's dark door,
Never did lie so low before,
Massa Jesus, He came riding by,
Oh! He gave me the wings for to rise and fly.—CHORUS.

3. When I was walking along one day,
I met an old hypocrite on my way,
She's always right and never is wrong,
She's always up and never is down,
Just watch that sun how study she runs,
Don't you never let her catch you with your work undone.—CHORUS.

4. You take your sister right by the hand,
And lead her 'long down in the Promise Land.
If my sister should have a fall,
Just get on your knees and carry 'er case to the Lord.—CHORUS.

Wm. H. Keyser & Co., Music Typographers, 921 Arch St., Phila

www.ingramcontent.com/pod-product-compliance
Lightning Source LLC
Chambersburg PA
CBHW021534270326

41930CB00008B/1241